50 Renaissance Solos for Classical Guitar

Arranged by Mark Phillips

PLAYBACK+
Speed • Pitch • Balance • Loop

To access audio visit:
www.halleonard.com/mylibrary

4698-3582-6581-0656

ISBN 978-1-57560-835-8

Visit Hal Leonard Online at
www.halleonard.com

Contents

Alman

Anonymous

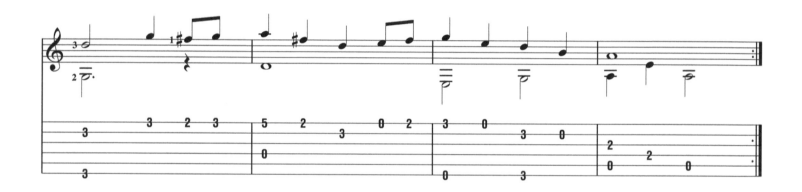

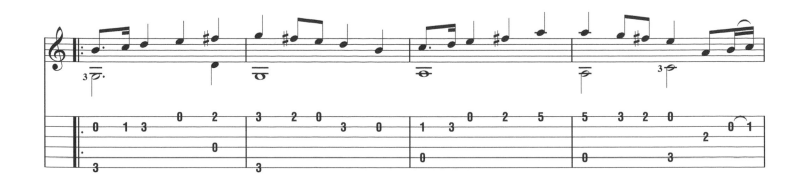

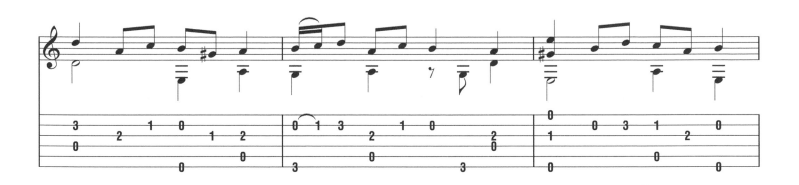

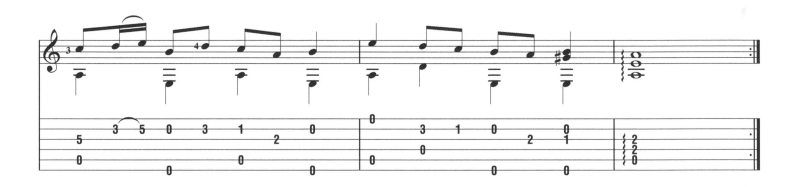

Alman I

Robert Johnson

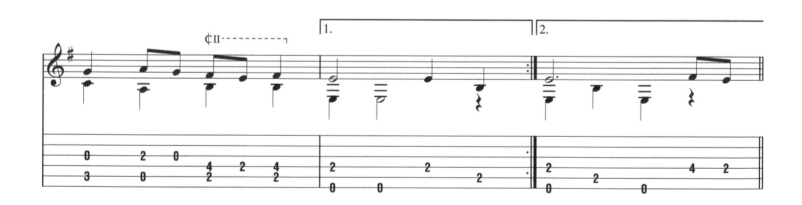

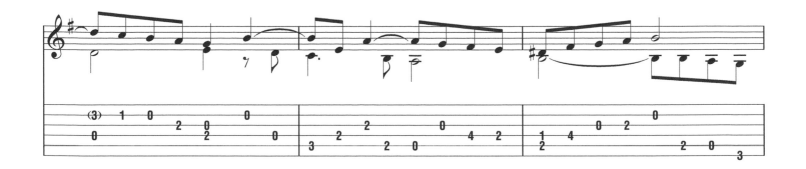

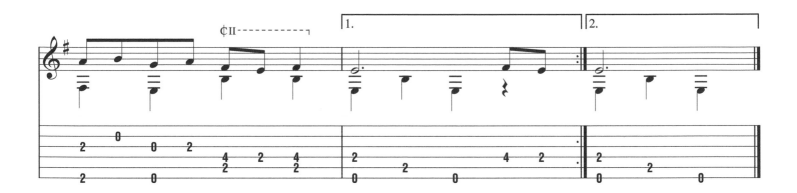

Alman II

Robert Johnson

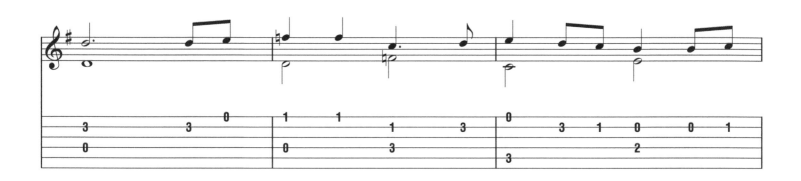

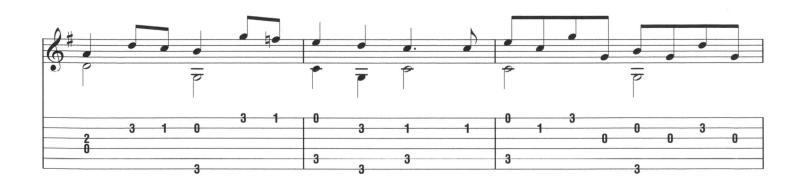

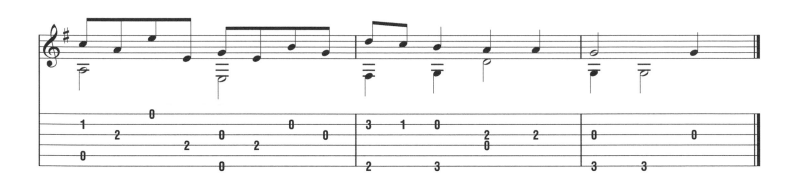

And Would You See My Mistress' Face

Philip Rosseter

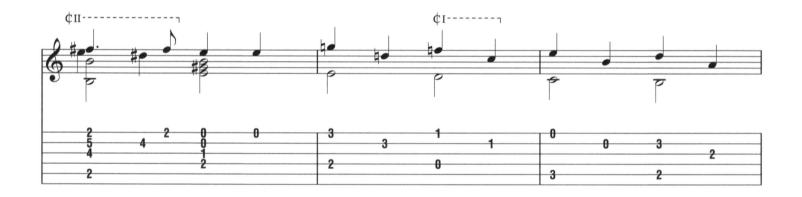

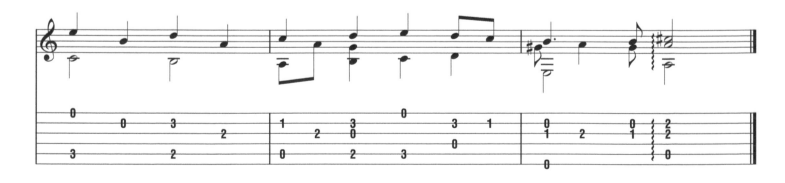

Away with These Selfe Loving Lads

John Dowland

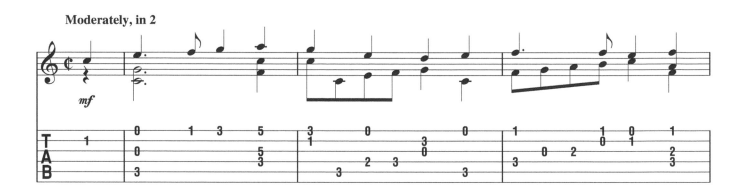

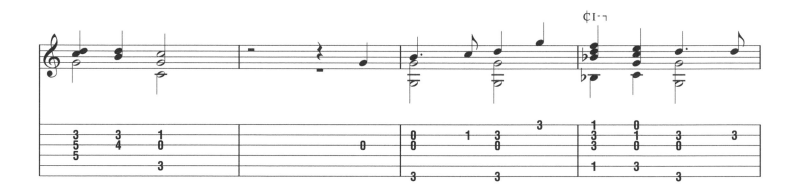

Ballet

John Sturt

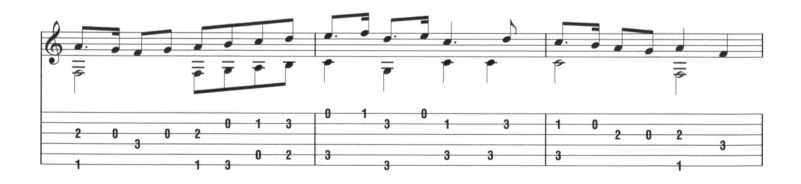

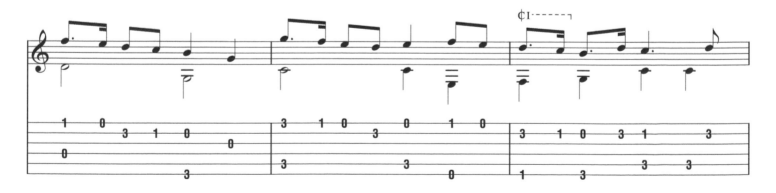

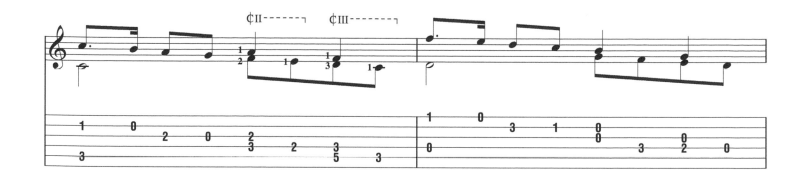

Corranto I

Anonymous

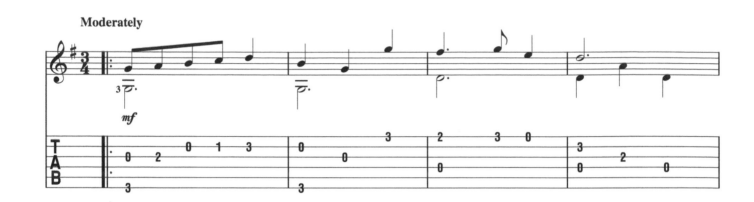

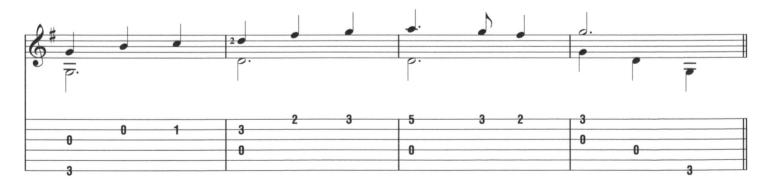

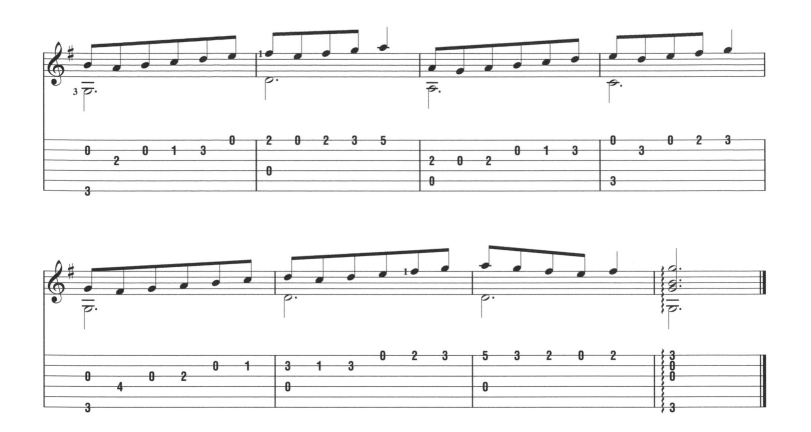

Corranto II

Anonymous

Moderately, in 2

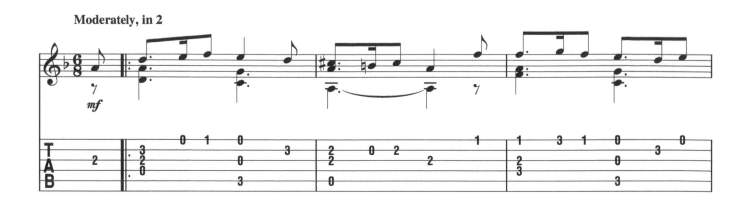

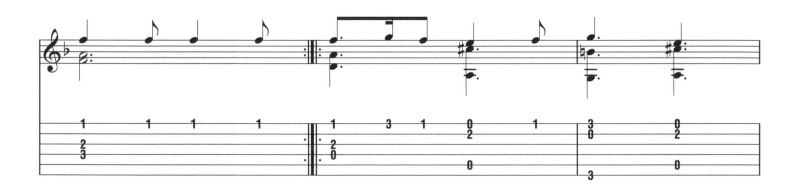

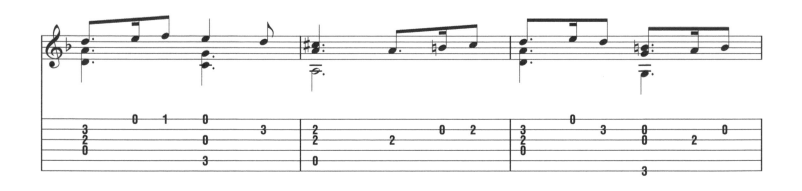

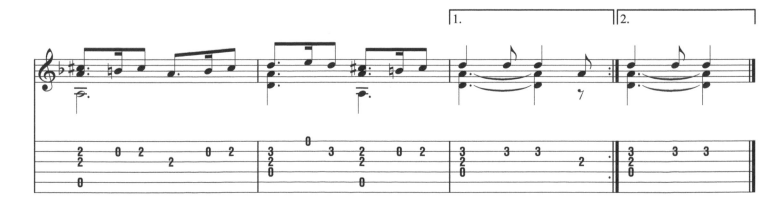

Coventry Carol

Anonymous

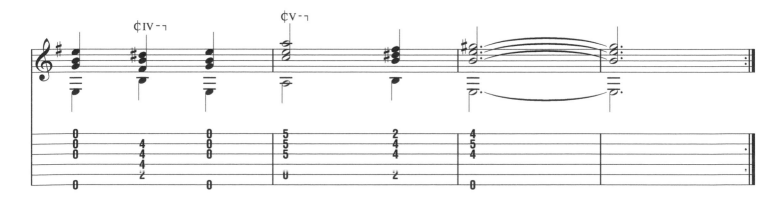

Curent

Anonymous

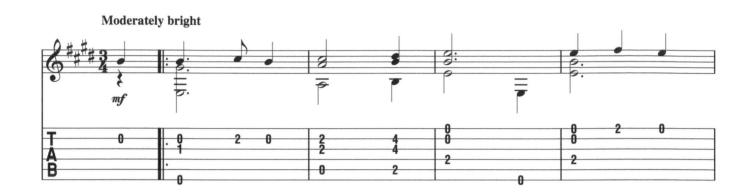

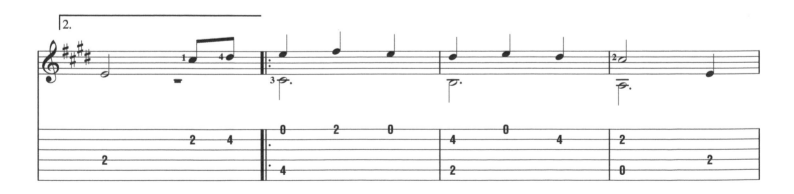

Dreame

Giles Farnaby

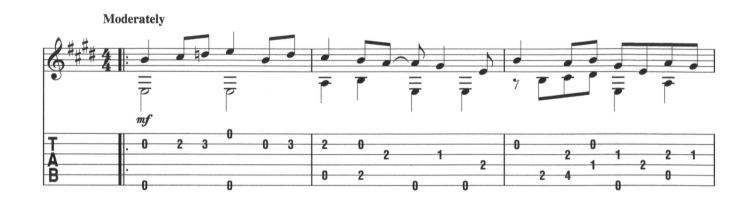

The Earl of Essex Gailliard

John Dowland

Moderately bright

Fine

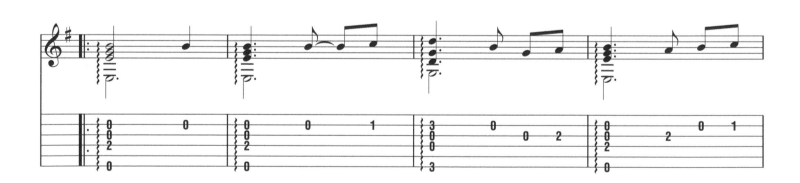

*2nd time, D.C.
(no repeat) al Fine*

Fayne Would I Wedd

Richard Farnaby

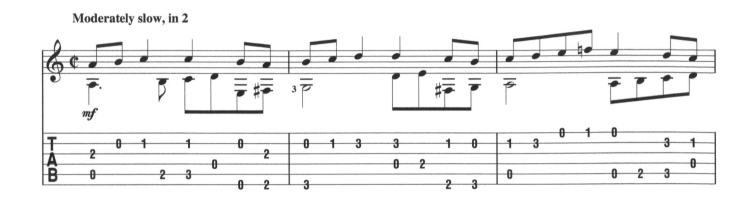

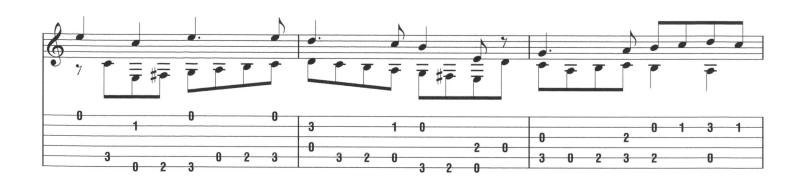

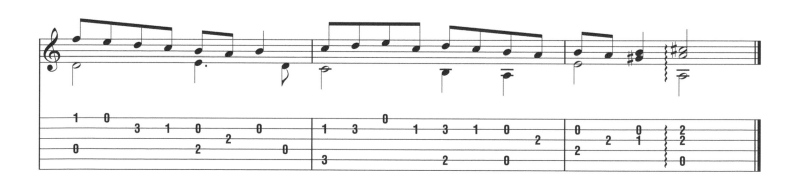

Everie Bush New Springing

Michaell Cavendish

The First Dance

Robert Johnson

Moderately

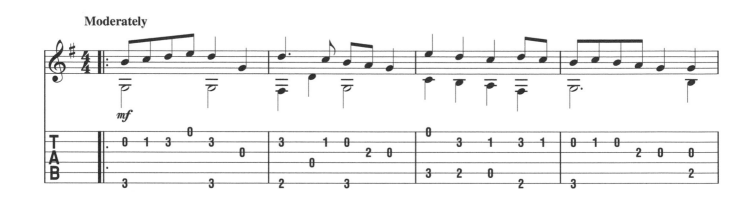

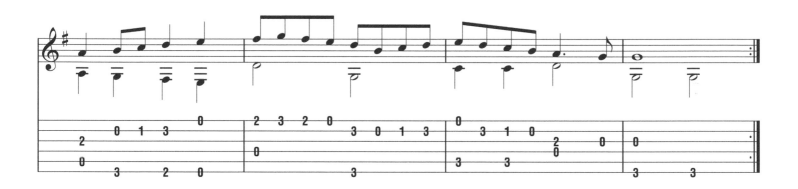

25

The Gillyflower

Anonymous

Moderately bright

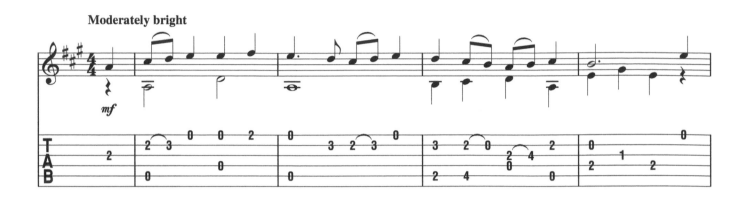

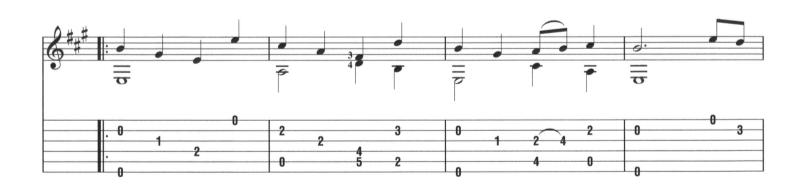

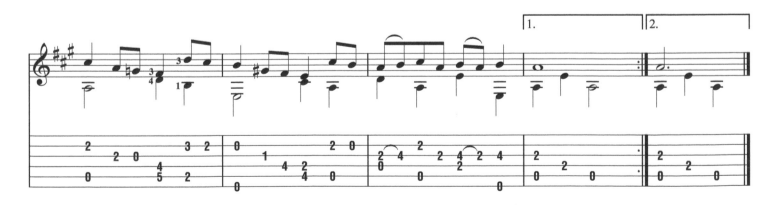

Go to Bed Sweete Muze

Robert Jones

Moderately slow, in 2

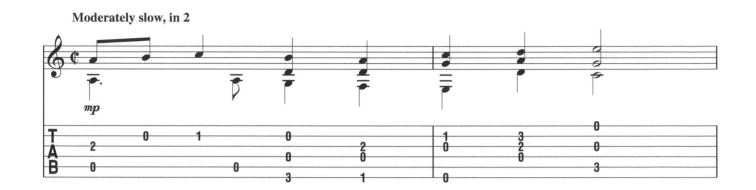

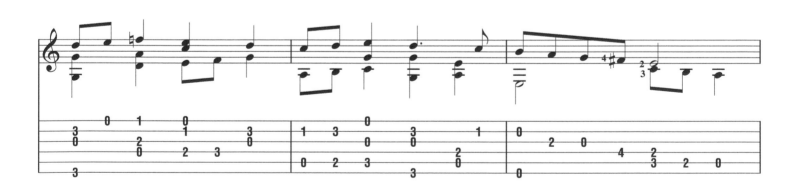

Home Again

Anonymous

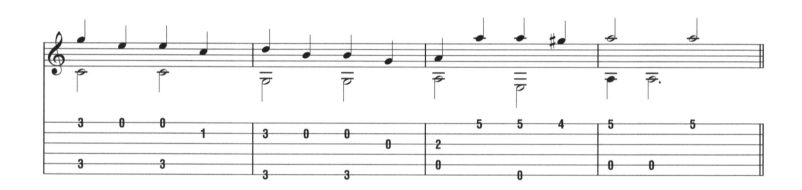

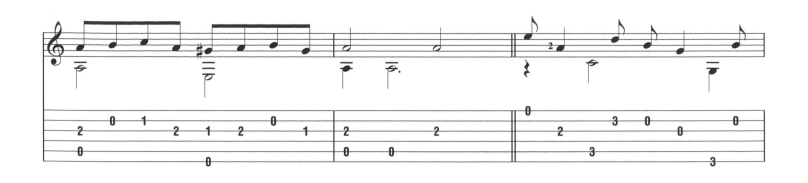

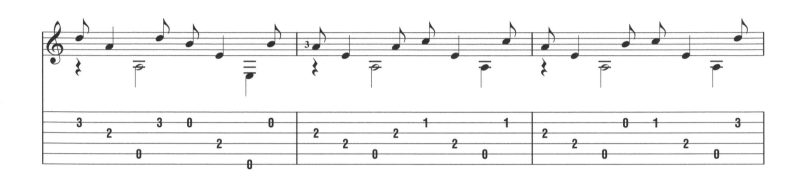

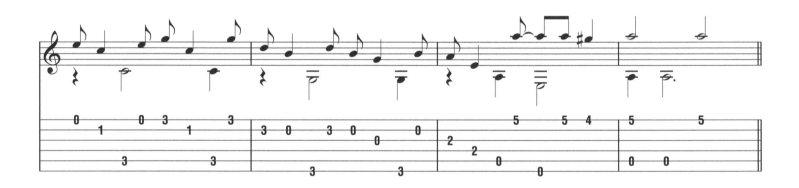

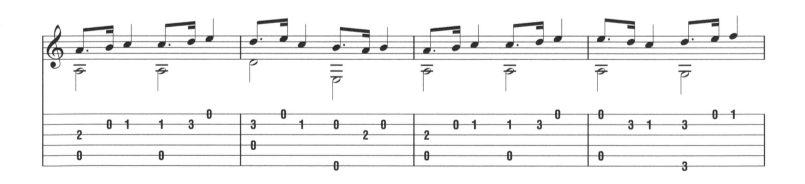

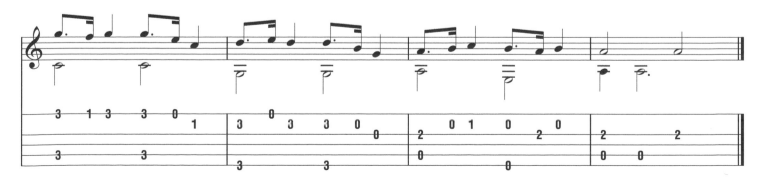

Greensleeves

Anonymous

Moderately slow, in 2

If Thou Longst So Much to Learne

Thomas Campian

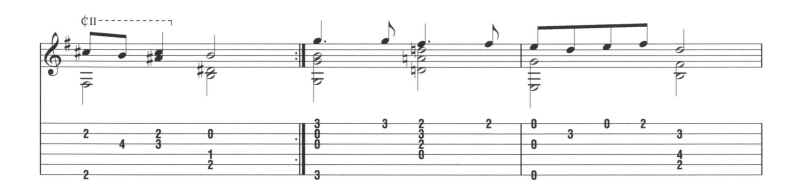

If You Were Mine

Anonymous

Moderately slow, in 2

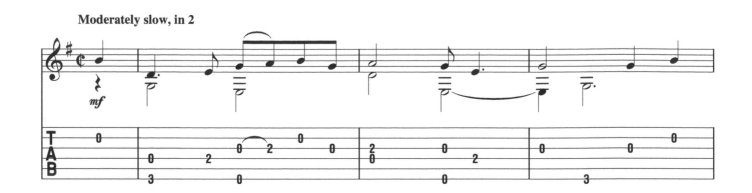

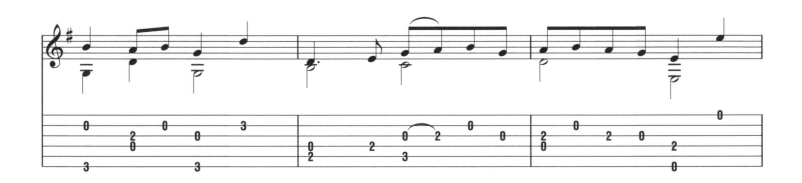

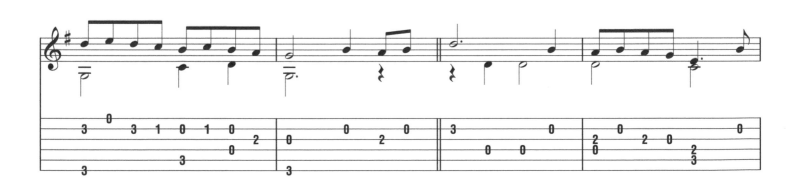

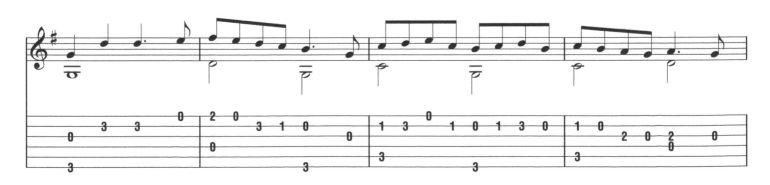

Jacke and Jone

Thomas Campian

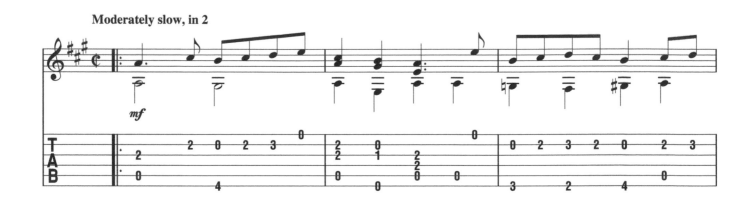

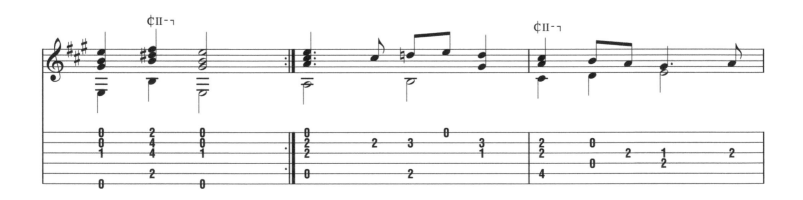

Lo, How a Rose E'er Blooming

Michael Praetorius

Slowly, gently, in 2

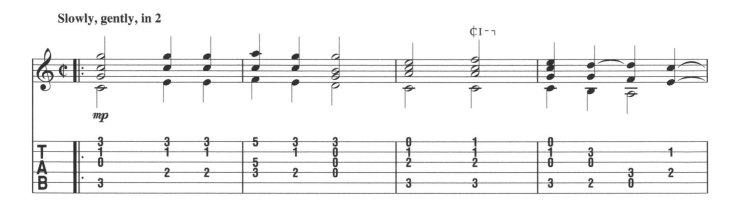

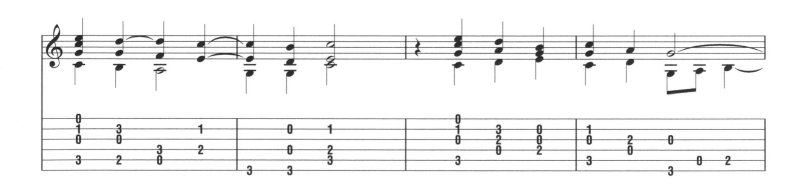

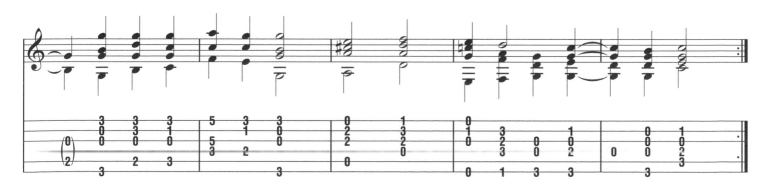

May

Thomas Robinson

Moderately slow, in 2

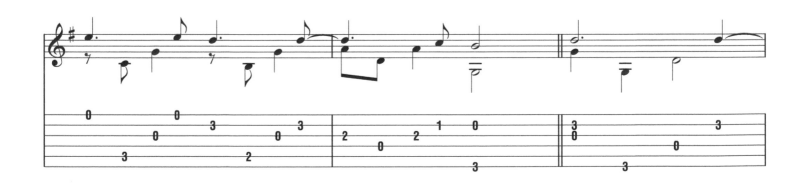

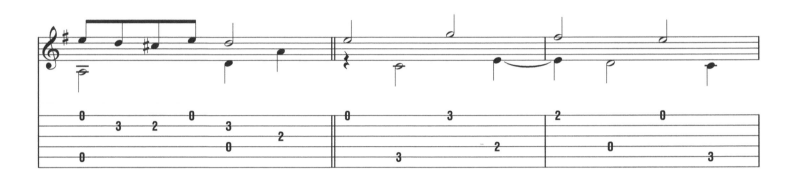

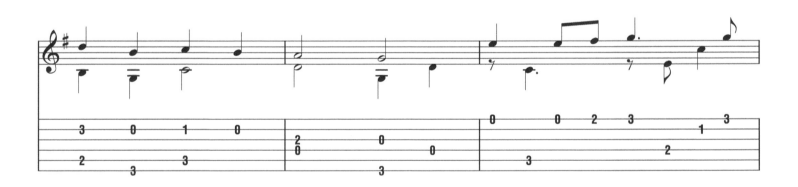

Lord Willoughby's Welcome Home

John Dowland

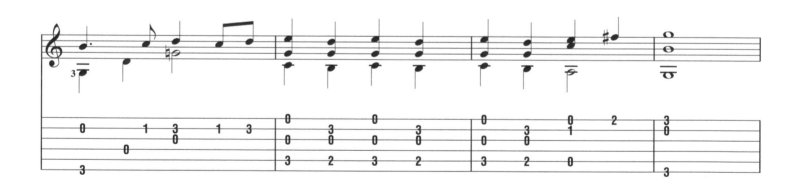

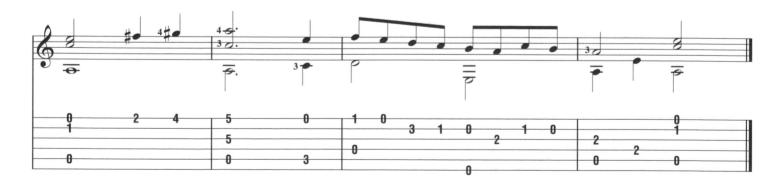

Never Weather-Beaten Saile

Thomas Campian

Moderately slow, in 2

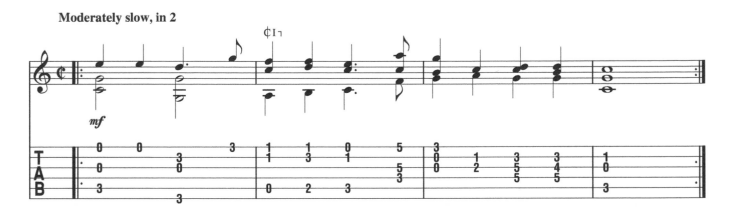

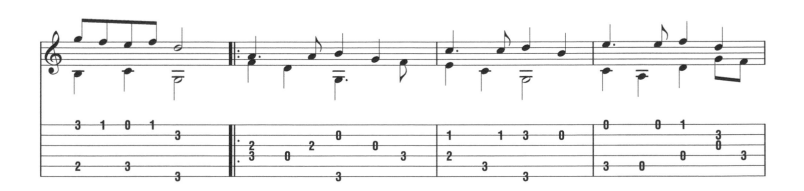

The Night Watch

Anthony Holborne

Moderately bright

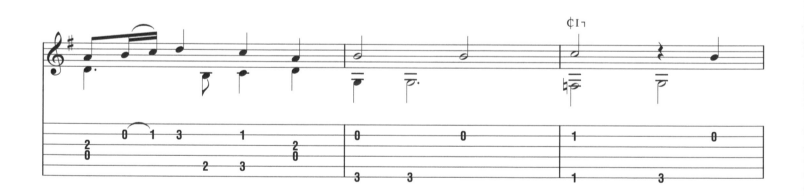

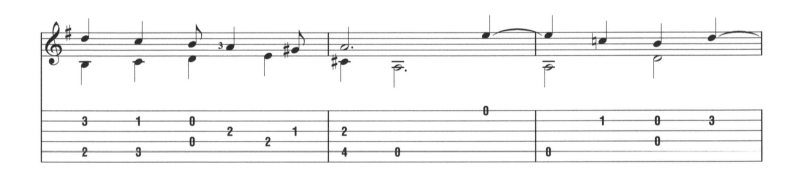

Packington's Pound

Anonymous

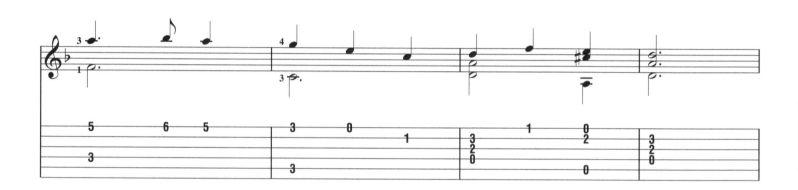

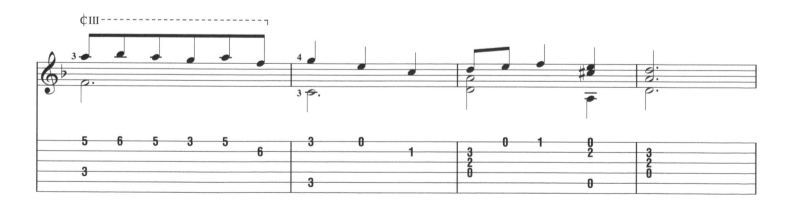

Now Winter Nights Enlarge

Thomas Campian

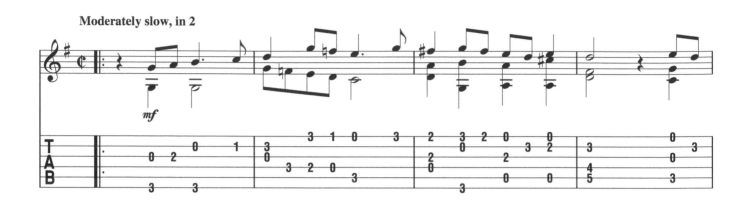

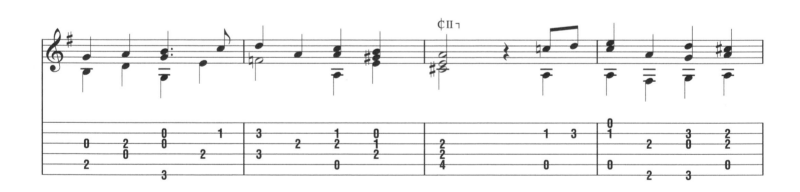

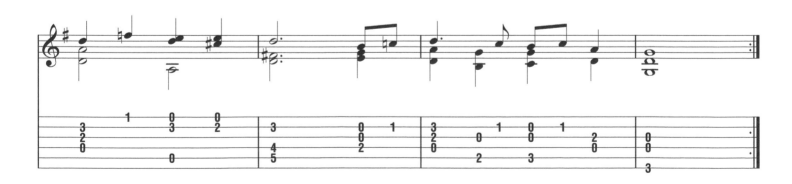

Passemese

Pierre Phalese

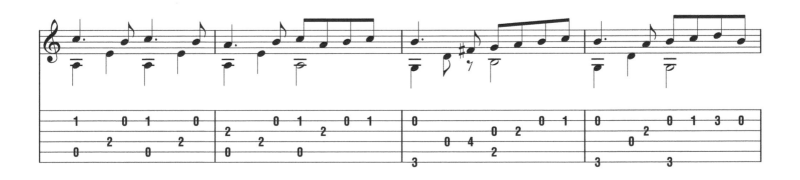

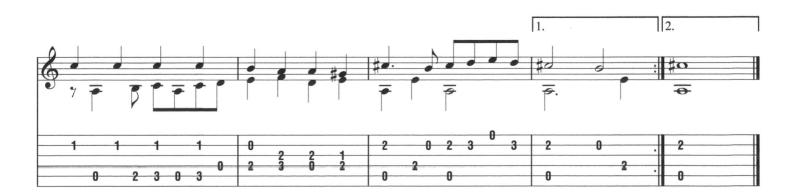

Pavana Muy Llana Para Tañer

Diego Pisador

Moderately

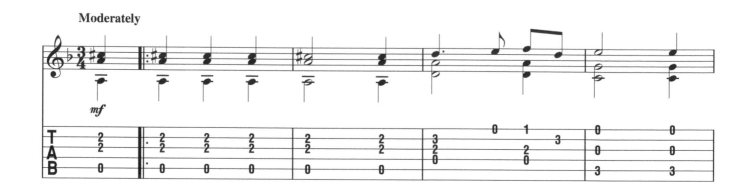

The Silver Swan

Orlando Gibbons

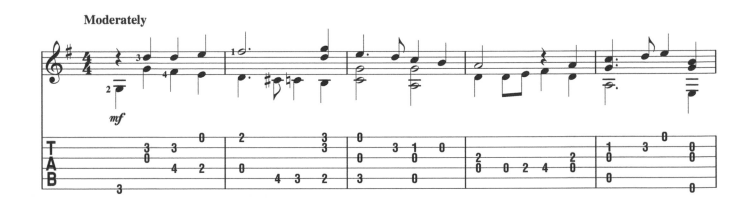

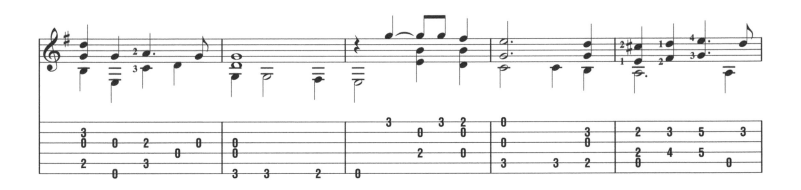

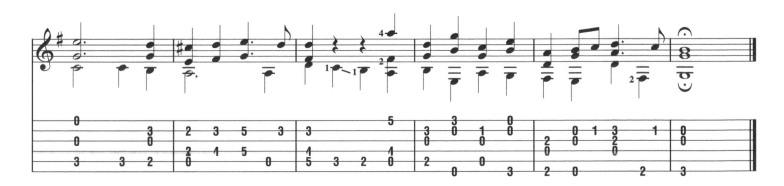

Soneto

Enriquez de Valderrabano

Moderately bright

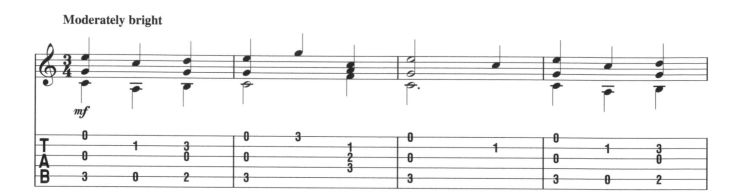

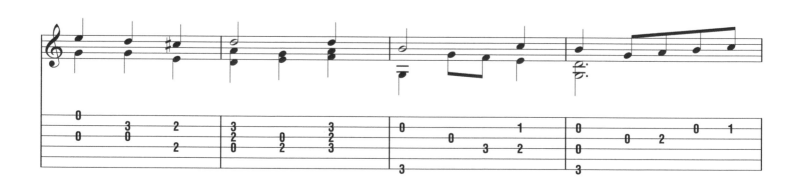

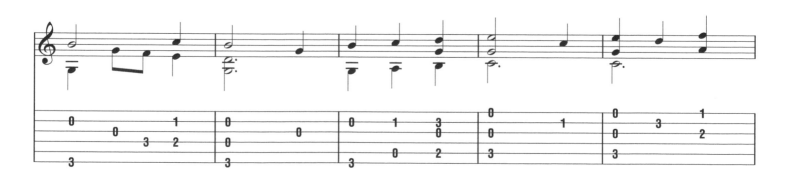

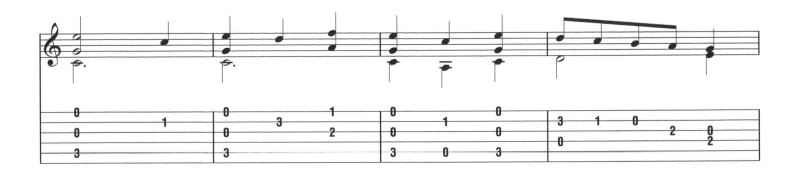

So Quick, So Hot, So Mad

Thomas Campian

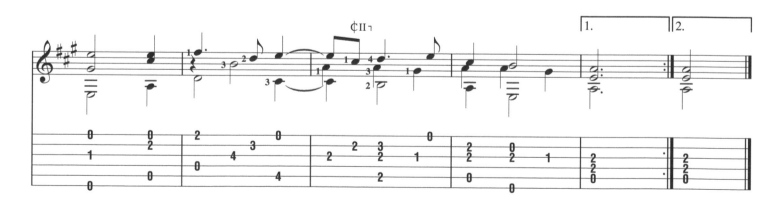

Tarleton's Resurrection

John Dowland

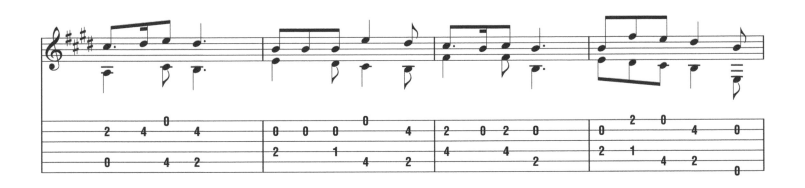

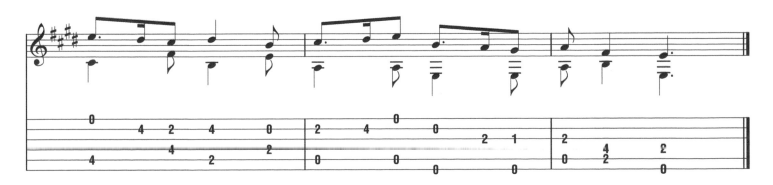

Think'st Thou to Seduce Me Then

Thomas Campian

Moderately slow, in 2

Though Your Strangeness Frets My Hart

Thomas Campian

Moderately slow, in 2

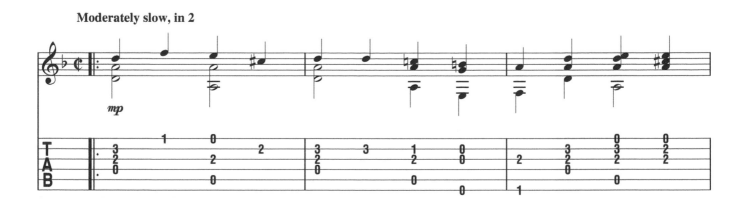

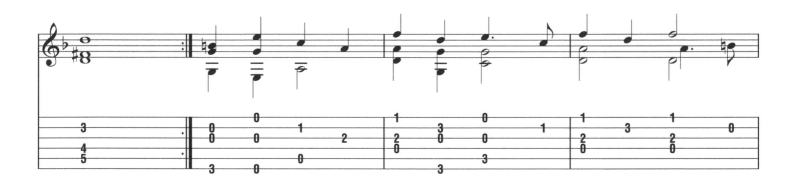

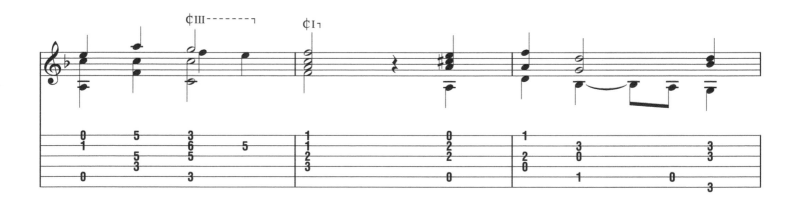

The Three Ravens

Thomas Ravenscroft

Moderately slow, in 2

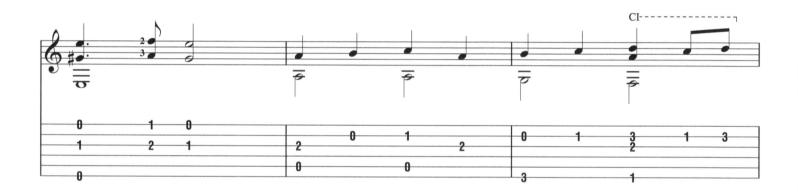

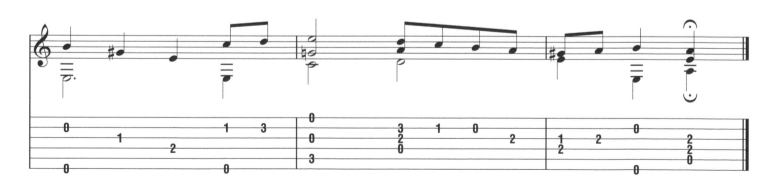

Thrice Tosse These Oaken Ashes

Thomas Campian

Moderately slow, in 2

To His Sweet Lute

Thomas Campian

Moderately slow, in 2

Toy

Francis Cutting

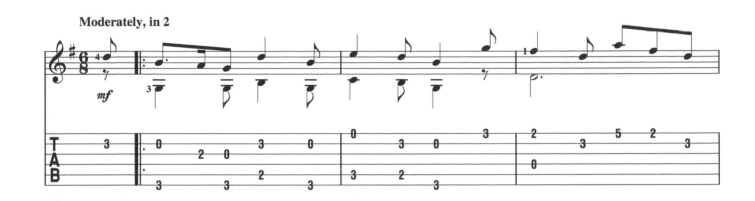

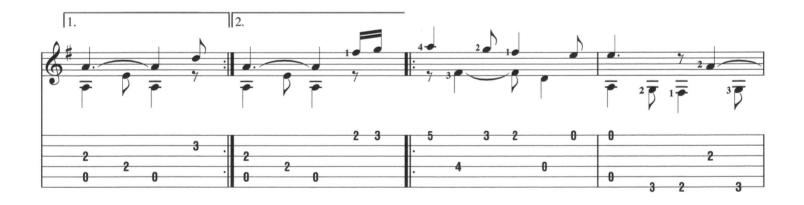

Turne Back You Wanton Flyer

Thomas Campian

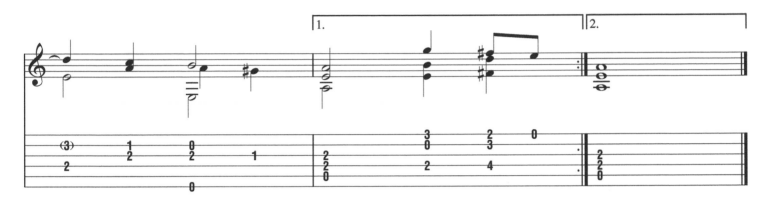

Under a Green Linden Tree

Nicolas Vallet

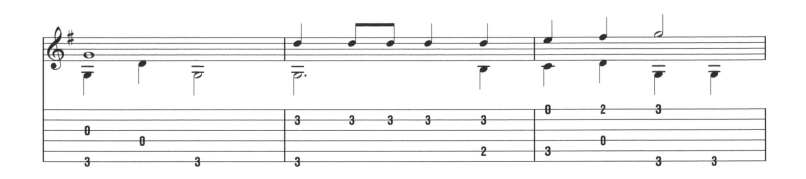

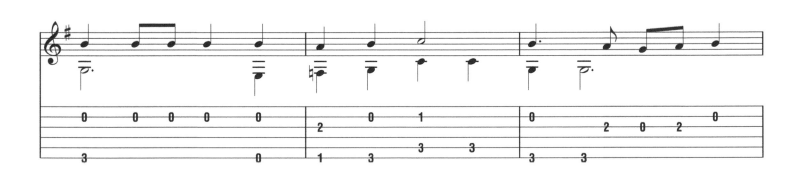

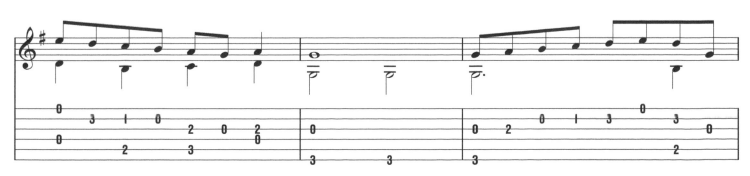

Watkins Ale

Anonymous

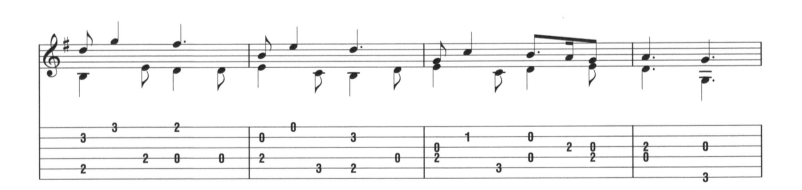

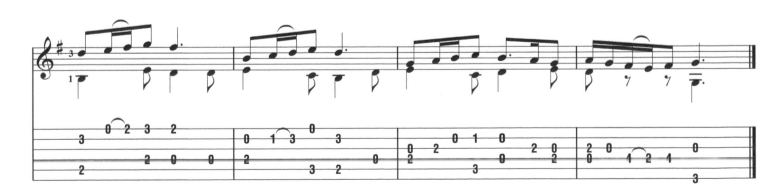

What Harvest Halfe So Sweet Is

Thomas Campian

Moderately slow, in 2

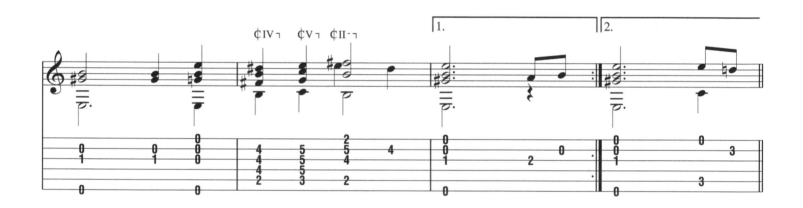

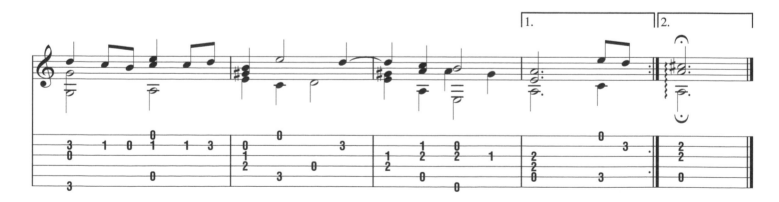

What Is a Day?

Philip Rosseter

Moderately

What Is Beauty But a Breath

Thomas Greaves

Slowly, in 2

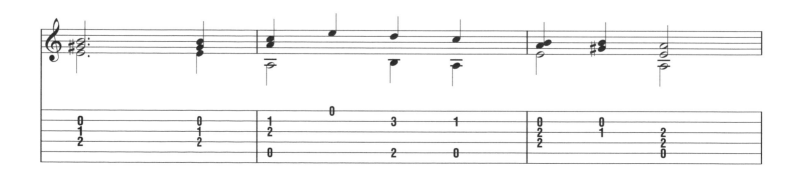

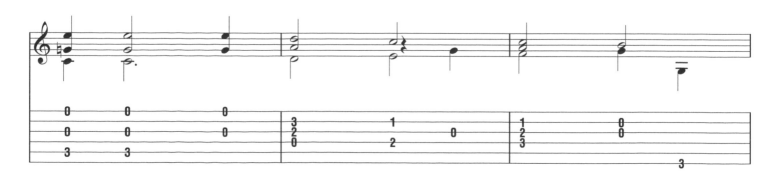

What Then Is Love

Thomas Ford

Slowly, in 1

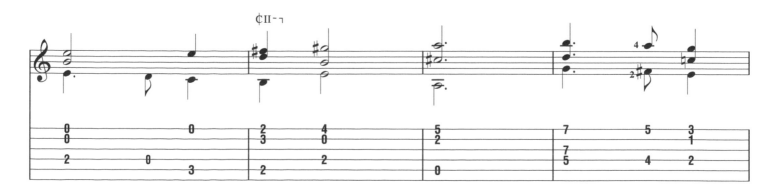

Wilson's Wilde

Anonymous

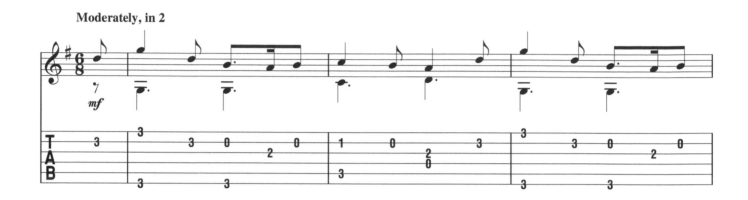

When Laura Smiles

Philip Rosseter

Slowly, in 1

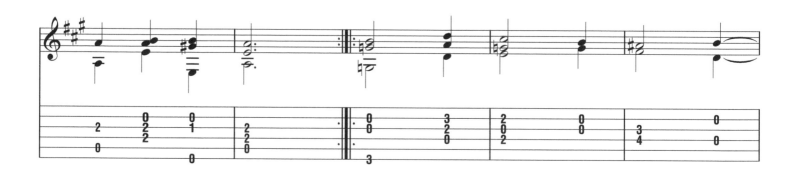